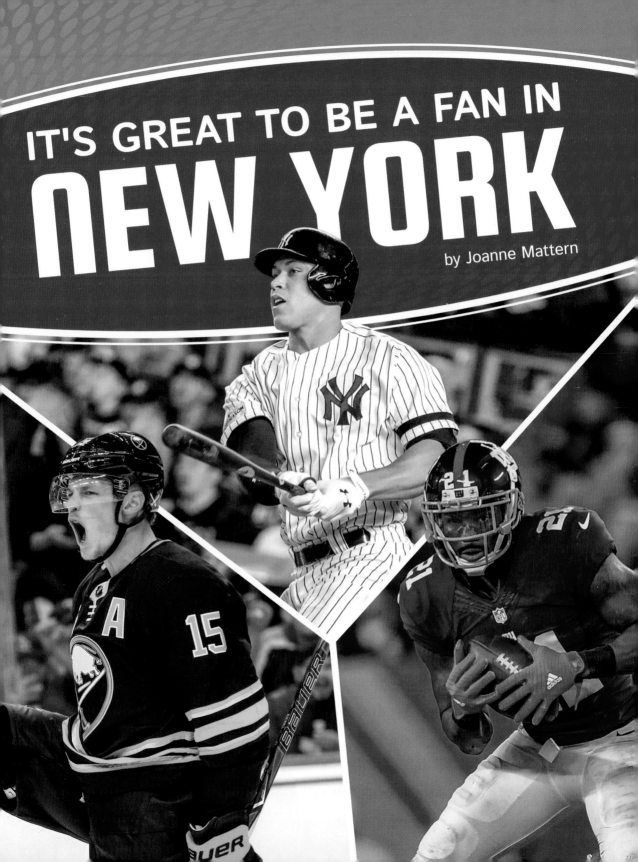

IT'S GREAT TO BE A FAN IN
NEW YORK

by Joanne Mattern

FOCUS READERS

www.focusreaders.com

Focus Readers is distributed by North Star Editions:
sales@northstareditions.com | 888-417-0195

Produced for Focus Readers by Red Line Editorial.

Photographs ©: Frank Franklin II/AP Images, cover (top), 1 (top); Jeffrey T. Barnes/AP Images, cover (bottom left), 1 (bottom left); Evan Pinkus/AP Images, cover (bottom right), 1 (bottom right); Osugi/Shutterstock Images, 4–5; Everett - Art/Shutterstock Images, 7; Red Line Editorial, 9, 21; ventdusud/Shutterstock Images, 11; AP Images, 12–13, 23, 37; Richard Cavalleri/Shutterstock Images, 15; Julie Jacobson/AP Images, 17; LM Otero/AP Images, 19; Alan Schwartz/Cal Sport Media/AP Images, 24–25; The World in HDR/Shutterstock Images, 27; Pabkov/Shutterstock Images, 28; Kevin Rivoli/AP Images, 31; a katz/Shutterstock Images, 32–33; Frank Romeo/Shutterstock Images, 34; eddtoro/Shutterstock Images, 38–39; Kathy Willens/AP Images, 43; Jason DeCrow/AP Image, 45

ISBN
978-1-63517-933-0 (hardcover)
978-1-64185-035-3 (paperback)
978-1-64185-237-1 (ebook pdf)
978-1-64185-136-7 (hosted ebook)

Library of Congress Control Number: 2018932000

Printed in the United States of America
Mankato, MN
May, 2018

ABOUT THE AUTHOR

Joanne Mattern has written more than 250 books for children and young adults. Her favorite topics are history, science, sports, and biography. Mattern is a New York native who loves the Yankees! She lives in the Hudson Valley with her husband, four children, and several pets.

TABLE OF CONTENTS

CHAPTER 1

A NEW YORK STATE OF MIND

New York is a land of mountains, beaches, big cities, farms, and more. Whatever the attraction, New York has it. That is true of sports as well. New York is a hotbed of sports teams and sports fans. The state is home to 10 teams in the four major North American sports, plus many more college and high school teams. And New Yorkers are some of the most passionate sports fans in the country.

The "Big Apple" of New York City is home to some of the most popular teams in the United States.

The first settlers in what is now New York were American Indians. Many different tribes lived in the area. Some of these tribes were the Delaware, Mohawk, Oneida, and Seneca. Several tribes came together as one nation to form the mighty Iroquois Confederacy.

The island of Manhattan, which is now part of New York City, was originally the home of the Lenape tribe. Manhattan comes from the Lenape word *mannahatta*, which means "land of many hills." Dutch merchants bought the land in 1626 and called it New Amsterdam. England took over in 1664 and added surrounding areas to create a larger British colony. The colony was named New York in honor of the Duke of York, a member of the English royal family.

As immigration from Europe increased, white settlers pushed the natives out. In many cases,

▲ The settlement of New Amsterdam looked quite different from the New York City of today.

this was done violently. In the mid-1700s, the French and Indian War claimed many native lives.

New York played a major role in the American Revolutionary War from 1775 to 1783. And after the US victory, New York was one of the original 13 states. It became a state on July 26, 1788.

Today, New York is 54,475 square miles (141,090 square km) in size. That makes it the 27th-largest state in the country in terms of area. The state can be divided into several regions.

The New York **metro** area surrounds New York City and its nearby suburbs. Just north of that is the Hudson Valley, with small towns lining the banks of the Hudson River. The Capital Region is centered in and around Albany, the state's capital city.

The Southern Tier and Central New York cover the middle part of the state. They are more **rural** than the eastern part of the state. The Finger Lakes and the Mohawk Valley regions are located in the central and western parts of the state. These areas have natural resources such as forests and lakes.

Each region of New York has its own culture and character. For example, life in central New York's dairy farm country is quiet and peaceful. But there is always something going on in noisy, crowded New York City. With a population of more than 8.5 million people, New York City is the largest city in the United States.

Other major cities in New York include the capital of Albany and the upstate cities of Buffalo, Rochester, and Syracuse. Most of New York's major cities have one or more colleges or universities.

MAP OF NEW YORK REGIONS ◄

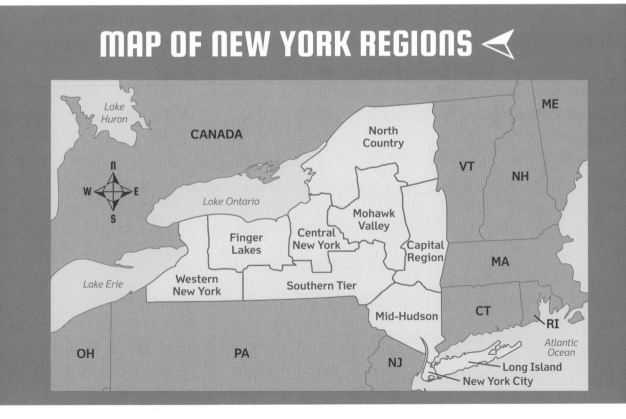

The financial industry is one of the biggest and most important industries in the state. New York City is home to the largest stock exchange in the United States. Many banks and financial companies have their headquarters in the city as well.

Other important industries include health care, professional services, retail, manufacturing, and education. New York's manufacturing industries produce a wide variety of products, including railroad cars, clothing, computers, and high-tech engineering tools.

Tourism is also a key part of the state's **economy**. Millions of visitors travel to New York each year to enjoy its natural beauty. They visit the world-famous Niagara Falls. They hike the Adirondack Mountains and the Hudson Valley. And New York City has a seemingly endless number

▲ The New York Stock Exchange is located on Wall Street in New York City.

of attractions, such as museums, shopping, and Broadway theater shows.

Sports are another major part of New York's economy and culture. In New York, sports are a huge part of everyday life. They are also a way to bring people together all over the state. New Yorkers take a great deal of pride in their state and their teams, and they are very loyal to both.

CHAPTER 2

AN EMPIRE OF TEAMS

Think of any sport, and it is probably played in New York. The first major league sport to come to New York was baseball. In 1857, the New York Mutuals became the state's first baseball team. But they disbanded in 1876.

Various other baseball teams have come and gone since then. Today the state has two teams. The New York Yankees have been there the longest.

The 1922 Giants won the World Series. But New York baseball history goes much further back.

The Yankees were originally called the Highlanders, but by 1913 they were known as the Yankees. The "Yanks" have won more World Series titles than any other team. They also boast some of the greatest players of all time, such as Babe Ruth, Mickey Mantle, Joe DiMaggio, Derek Jeter, and Mariano Rivera.

In 1958, two of the state's baseball teams moved to California. They were the Brooklyn Dodgers and the New York Giants. But in 1962, another baseball team arrived. The New York Metropolitans, or Mets, began playing in New York City. They won World Series titles in 1969 and 1986.

New Yorkers love baseball, but they love football, too. New York's first pro football team was the Giants, who began playing in 1925. The Giants originally played at the Polo Grounds in

The Jets and Giants share MetLife Stadium in East Rutherford, New Jersey.

Manhattan. Later, they played at Yankee Stadium in the Bronx. In 1976, they moved to a stadium in New Jersey, just a few miles west of New York City.

Another New York football team, the Jets, began playing in 1960 at the Polo Grounds. They were originally known as the New York Titans. But in 1963, they moved to Shea Stadium near LaGuardia Airport and changed their name to the Jets.

In 1984, the Jets moved to New Jersey to share a stadium with the Giants. Though the Jets and Giants both play in New Jersey, residents of New York City are still passionate about the teams.

Not all of the state's football teams are in the New York City metro. The Bills have played upstate in Buffalo since their founding in 1960. During the 1990s, they went to four Super Bowls in a row. Unfortunately, they lost all four.

Basketball is another popular sport in New York, although the action centers on New York City. That's where all the state's professional teams play.

The National Basketball Association (NBA) formed in 1946. One of the original teams was the New York Knickerbockers, whose name was later shortened to the Knicks. The Knickerbockers played in the NBA's very first game. Today,

▲ Forward Kristaps Porzingis thrills Knicks fans with his dunking ability.

the team plays in the famous Madison Square Garden. The arena is also home to the New York Liberty. This team is part of the Women's National Basketball Association (WNBA). The Liberty have been in the WNBA since the league's first season in 1996.

The Nets have played in the New York area since 1967. However, they have had many different names and homes. The team began play as the New Jersey Americans. At that time, they were part of the American Basketball Association (ABA). When the ABA went out of business, the newly named Nets joined the NBA in 1976. They moved around a lot over the years, playing in both New York and New Jersey. In 2012, they moved to the Barclays Center in Brooklyn and changed their name to the Brooklyn Nets.

New York fans also love sports on ice. The state is home to three National Hockey League (NHL) teams. The oldest of these teams is the New York Rangers. But they were not the first hockey team to play in New York City. That honor goes to the New York Americans, who started playing in 1925. The Americans played at Madison Square Garden.

▲ NHL legend Wayne Gretzky played his last three seasons in a Rangers uniform from 1996 to 1999.

The team did so well that the owner of the Garden wanted a team of his own. So he created the New York Rangers. The Rangers played their first game in 1926, and they still play at the Garden today.

The Americans went out of business in 1942. That left the Rangers as the only major pro hockey team in New York City for several decades. But that all changed in the 1970s.

In 1972, the New York Islanders joined the NHL. The Islanders won four Stanley Cups in a row from 1980 to 1983. It took the Rangers more than 65 years to win that many.

Many parts of New York are cold and icy in the winter, so it's natural that fans outside the city love hockey as well. Upstate New York is represented by the Buffalo Sabres. The Sabres were an NHL expansion team in 1970.

The New York metro area also has two pro soccer teams. The New York Red Bulls were an original team when Major League Soccer (MLS) began playing in 1996. At the time, they were

> **THINK ABOUT IT**
>
> Do you think having more than one team benefits a city? Why or why not?

known as the New York/New Jersey MetroStars. A new team called New York City FC played its first game in 2015. NYCFC plays at Yankee Stadium, while the Red Bulls play in New Jersey.

NEW YORK'S CHAMPIONS

New York Yankees	27 World Series
New York Giants	4 Super Bowls
New York Islanders	4 Stanley Cups
New York Rangers	4 Stanley Cups
New York Knicks	2 NBA championships
New York Mets	2 World Series
New York Jets	1 Super Bowl

Accurate as of January 2018.

LOU GEHRIG

Lou Gehrig was one of the greatest baseball players in history. His strength and determination led to his nickname, the "Iron Horse." Gehrig was born to a poor family in Manhattan in 1903. The New York Yankees signed him in 1923. Playing first base, Gehrig was an excellent fielder and an even better hitter. In 1931, he set a record with 184 runs batted in. In 1932, he became only the third player to hit four home runs in a single game. In World Series games, Gehrig batted .361 and led the team to six championships. But Gehrig's most amazing record was playing in 2,130 straight games between 1925 and 1939.

His streak ended only because he fell ill during the 1938 season. In June 1939, he was diagnosed with a neurological disease called ALS. Today, this disease is also known as Lou Gehrig's disease. Gehrig was forced to retire from baseball

△ On June 2, 1925, Lou Gehrig started at first base for the Yankees and didn't miss another game until 1939.

immediately. The Yankees honored him with "Lou Gehrig Day" at Yankee Stadium. Gehrig's uniform No. 4 was retired, and he gave a speech in front of more than 61,000 fans. Despite his diagnosis, Gehrig called himself "the luckiest man on the face of the Earth." Gehrig died in 1941, but he is still remembered today as one of the best players in baseball history.

CHAPTER 3

THE BIG-TICKET WORLD OF COLLEGE SPORTS

Along with its professional teams, New York also has many strong college teams. The best teams in the state play in **Division I** of the National Collegiate Athletic Association (NCAA).

Basketball is one of the most popular college sports in New York. The state has 22 Division I men's teams. Historically, the best team in the state has been the Syracuse University Orange. They usually reach the NCAA Tournament.

Syracuse University's sports teams are called the Orange, and fans dress appropriately.

Other top teams in the state include Cornell University, Siena College, Iona College, and St. John's University. There are many women's Division I teams as well. In 2016, Syracuse became the first New York team to make a women's Final Four.

College football has a long history in New York. The state was among the first to have football as a college sport. In 1870, Columbia University in New York City became the third college football team ever. The **rivalry** between the Army team in West Point and the Navy team in Maryland goes back to 1890 and is still a hot contest each year.

Today, football continues to rule at many of New York's colleges. Syracuse, Army, and Fordham University are three of the state's most successful teams. In addition to the top Division I teams, many schools offer sports in the NCAA's

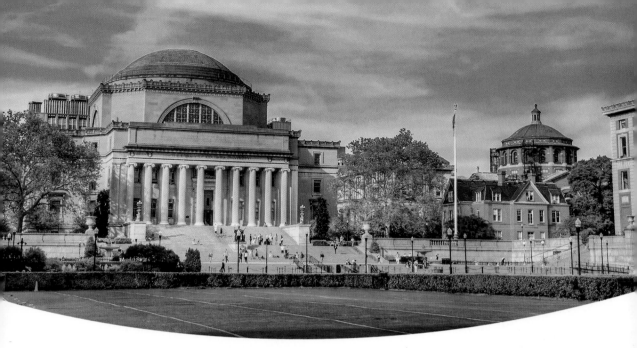

Columbia University in Manhattan is the state's oldest college and has the state's oldest football program.

Division II and Division III. These levels are for smaller schools, but the games themselves are just as **competitive**.

New York is a destination for college basketball fans around the country. Madison Square Garden hosts the Big East Tournament and the men's National Invitation Tournament (NIT). The NIT is the oldest college basketball tournament in the country.

▲ Madison Square Garden is the home of St. John's basketball and the final round of the NIT.

A strong athletic program is very important to many colleges. Schools are eager to **recruit** top athletes. They often offer generous **scholarships** to students to play on college teams. For example, Syracuse has a great reputation as a top sports school. The school's competitive teams and record of national championships make it a top choice both for student athletes and for students who are sports fans.

College teams also add money to the local economy. Tens of thousands of fans go to games. They spend money at restaurants and hotels in the area. They also buy team **merchandise**. This brings more money to the school and to local businesses.

When it comes to sports, college teams can be a big business. They can also be a great source of pride to New York fans. These schools represent communities that love to cheer them on.

THINK ABOUT IT ◄

What are the benefits of going to a school with a powerful and famous sports team?

CARMELO ANTHONY

Carmelo Anthony is an NBA superstar and one of the best scorers in the league. Anthony has many ties to New York. He was born in Brooklyn in 1984. However, soon after he moved to Baltimore, Maryland, where he became one of the best high school players in the nation.

Anthony returned to New York for college. He attended Syracuse during the 2002–03 season. As a freshman, Anthony became the school's best player. In 2003, he led the Orangemen to their first national championship.

After one year of college, Anthony felt he was ready to join the NBA. He was drafted by the Denver Nuggets. Anthony played for the Nuggets between 2003 and 2011. Then, in the middle of the 2011 season, he was traded to the New York Knicks.

Carmelo Anthony led Syracuse to the national championship in his one season of college basketball.

Back home in New York, Anthony became a fan favorite. Known as "Melo," he excelled playing at the forward position. During the 2012–13 season, Anthony scored at least 20 points in 31 straight games. This achievement broke a 51-year-old team record. Anthony remained with the Knicks until 2017, when he was traded to Oklahoma City to play for the Thunder.

CHAPTER 4

HOST TO CHAMPIONS

In addition to its famous sports teams, New York has hosted many important sporting events. The state is home to the New York City Marathon, which is held every year on the first weekend in November. Athletes come from all over the world to compete in this prestigious race.

New York City also hosts the US Open tennis championships every summer. Nearly 700,000 people turned out in 2017 to watch the action.

Nearly 100,000 people applied to run the New York City Marathon in 2017.

Arthur Ashe Stadium hosts the final of the US Open and is the largest tennis stadium in the world.

The tournament is held in Forest Hills, Queens, with the final at Arthur Ashe Stadium.

Horse racing fans come out to watch the Belmont Stakes every June. The third leg of the Triple Crown is held at a racetrack just outside New York City.

No event is bigger or more international than the Olympic Games. As the site of two Olympic Winter Games, Lake Placid has seen some amazing moments. The small town in upstate New York hosted the Winter Games for the first time in 1932. A total of 252 athletes, 231 men and 21 women, competed in 14 events.

Perhaps the most famous athlete to compete at the 1932 Games was Sonja Henie from Norway. Henie had won a gold medal for figure skating in 1928 when she was 15 years old. She defended her title at Lake Placid and delighted audiences with her incredible skill.

The 1932 Games also saw the **debut** of women's speed skating as a demonstration sport at the Olympics. All of the athletes who competed were from the United States or Canada. They competed in a format called "pack-style," in which all the skaters started at the same time.

In 1980, the Olympic Winter Games made a return to Lake Placid. It was still a small town, but the Games had gotten bigger and better. This time, 1,072 athletes competed in 38 events.

The 1980 Games produced some amazing moments and records.

American speed skater Eric Heiden was one of the stars. Heiden entered five events and won the gold medal in all five. He became the first Olympian to win five gold medals in individual events in the same Games.

The most dramatic event at the 1980 Olympics occurred in men's ice hockey. For years, the Soviet Union had dominated the sport. Its players had trained for years like a professional team and were considered the best in the world. The US team, on the other hand, was made up of college

➤ THINK ABOUT IT

None of New York's major cities has hosted the Olympic Games. Do you think New York City would be a good Olympic host city? Why or why not?

▲ The 1980 "Miracle on Ice" was one of the most famous moments in American sports history.

players who lacked international experience. Just three days before the Games, the Soviets had defeated the Americans 10–3 in an **exhibition**. But somehow, the US team defeated the Soviets 4–3 in Lake Placid. The victory became known as the "Miracle on Ice." Many people have called it the most exciting moment in sports history. Team USA went on to win the gold medal by beating Finland 4–2 two days later.

CHAPTER 5

NEW YORK SPORTS LIFE

Sports are fun to watch and fun to play. However, they also can be a huge business. New York's professional teams are worth billions of dollars. And while it is expensive to own and run a professional sports team, the teams also generate a huge amount of money.

The Yankees are one of the most popular teams in the world. They are also one of the most valuable. In 2017, they were worth $3.7 billion.

Opened in 2009, the new Yankee Stadium was one of the most expensive stadiums ever built.

Several other New York teams were also valued at more than $1 billion. The Knicks were the world's most valuable basketball team.

A team's value is made up of many elements. Much of the money comes from fans. Fans buy

➤ VALUE AND REVENUE OF NEW YORK TEAMS AS OF 2017

Team	Current Value ($ million)	Revenue ($ million)
New York Yankees	$3,700	$526
New York Knicks	$3,600	$426
New York Giants	$3,300	$477
New York Jets	$2,750	$431
Brooklyn Nets	$2,300	$273
New York Mets	$2,000	$332
Buffalo Bills	$1,600	$352
New York Rangers	$1,500	$246
New York Islanders	$395	$110
Buffalo Sabres	$350	$120

tickets to the games. They also support their teams by buying merchandise and souvenirs. Going to a major sporting event is not cheap. Tickets often cost more than $100 each. And of course, while they are at the game, fans buy food and drinks, generating even more revenue for the team.

Teams also earn a lot of money through broadcasting rights. Television, internet, and other media companies pay billions of dollars to broadcast games. Teams also earn money through sponsorships and advertising. And they get a portion of merchandise sales as well.

Not all sporting events in New York involve major teams like the Yankees or the Nets. Minor league teams also provide fun for fans at a much lower price. Minor league baseball teams can be found all over the state, from Brooklyn to Buffalo.

Spectators might even see a future star at the beginning of his or her career.

New York fans can also get a close look at their favorite pro football teams. All three New York teams hold their training camps at local colleges. The Giants practice at the University of Albany. The Jets have practiced at the State University at Cortland. The Bills practice at St. John Fisher College near Rochester. Fans love to attend these practices. They get to see their favorite players up close and have a good chance of meeting them and getting autographs. Once again, these fans add money to the local economy by buying souvenirs and visiting local restaurants or staying at a local hotel. Following teams closely is a big part of New York sports culture.

Along with the economic benefits of having a major sports team in the area, sports are an

important part of life for New Yorkers. Fans support their team in good seasons and bad. A person's favorite team can become an important part of who they are. Fans band together to support their team and have rivalries with fans of other teams. People identify as a Yankees fan or a Mets fan, as a Giants fan or a Jets fan. The annual Subway Series between the Yankees and Mets determines which team rules New York baseball.

New Yorkers may share one metro area, but they are intensely loyal to their favorite teams. And even though the Giants and the Jets play at the same stadium, their fans would probably never attend a game featuring the other team.

Champions are honored with parades. One of the biggest honors that a New York City sports team can have is a ticker-tape parade through the streets of lower Manhattan. These city blocks are called the "Canyon of Heroes," and it is a thrilling experience for fans to see their team in such a parade. Championship athletes and teams also receive the keys to the city. And fans turn out

> **THINK ABOUT IT**

What are some of the drawbacks to having a major sports team in a city or town?

New York's championship teams, like the 2009 Yankees, receive the honor of a parade down the Canyon of Heroes.

by the thousands to welcome their heroes home after a win. These fans have pride in their team and pride in their state. Sports teams in New York have given fans plenty to cheer for.

FOCUS ON
NEW YORK

Write your answers on a separate piece of paper.

1. Write a sentence that describes the economic benefits to a city of having a sports team, as discussed in Chapter 5.

2. Which is your favorite New York sports team? Why?

3. What was the original name of the New York Yankees?

     A. Highlanders
     B. Metropolitans
     C. Dodgers

4. Why are the Yankees one of the most valuable teams in the world?

     A. They play in New York City.
     B. Baseball teams are always the most valuable.
     C. They make a lot of money and have worldwide popularity.

Answers key on page 48.

GLOSSARY

competitive
Having a strong desire to win in a sport or other activity.

debut
First appearance.

Division I
The top level of college sports in the United States.

economy
A system of goods, services, money, and jobs.

exhibition
A game in which the result does not count toward the regular season standings.

merchandise
Manufactured goods that are bought and sold.

metro
The area around a city; short for "metropolitan."

recruit
To seek out new members for a group or activity.

rivalry
An ongoing competition between two players or teams.

rural
Having to do with the countryside.

scholarships
Money given to students to pay for educational expenses.

TO LEARN MORE

BOOKS

Appel, Martin. *Pinstripe Pride: The Inside Story of the New York Yankees*. New York: Simon & Schuster, 2015.

Burgan, Michael. *Miracle on Ice: How a Stunning Upset United a Country*. Mankato, MN: Compass Point Books, 2016.

Jackson, Aurelia. *Carmelo Anthony*. Broomall, PA: Mason Crest, 2015.

NOTE TO EDUCATORS

Visit **www.focusreaders.com** to find lesson plans, activities, links, and other resources related to this title.

INDEX

Answer Key: 1. Answers will vary; **2.** Answers will vary; **3.** A; **4.** C